THE
BUNK BED
BOOK

To William,
this is your book as much as it is mine.

FIRST EDITION
26 25 24 23 22   5 4 3 2 1

Text © 2022 Laura Fenton

Cover photograph courtesy of Benjamin Moore
Back cover photograph by Peter Dolkas

Published by Gibbs Smith
P.O. Box 667, Layton, Utah 84041

1.800.835.4993 orders
www.gibbs-smith.com

Designed by Ryan Thomann
Printed and bound in China

Gibbs Smith books are printed on either recycled, 100% post-consumer
waste, FSC-certified papers or on paper produced from sustainable
PEFC-certified forest/controlled wood source. Learn more at www.pefc.org.

Library of Congress Cataloging-in-Publication Data

Names: Fenton, Laura, 1980– author.
Title: The bunk bed book : 115 bunks, lofts, and cozy nooks / Laura Fenton.
Identifiers: LCCN 2021022512 | ISBN 9781423657330 (hardcover) |
ISBN 9781423657347 (epub)
Subjects: LCSH: Bunk beds.
Classification: LCC NK2713 .F46 2021 | DDC 749/.3—dc23
LC record available at https://lccn.loc.gov/2021022512

CONTENTS

introduction

EVERYONE LOVES A BUNK BED

Whether you are five or sixty-five, there is something about a cozy sleeping nook that excites the imagination. Have you ever noticed how children seek out small enclosures? They crawl under tables, hide in closets, and make blanket forts to create their own kid-size worlds. Or have you felt the feeling of joy that you get when you sit in a high-up perch? Looking down from a treehouse, we naturally gain a fresh perspective and an everyday feeling of transcendence. Or perhaps you've felt the comfort of an afternoon spent curled up with an engrossing book in a quiet corner? Bunk beds and enclosed sleeping nooks satiate some of our most universal longings: our love for secret places, the feeling of being aloft, and the comfort of enclosure.

After my first book, *The Little Book of Living Small*, was published, my then four-year-old son William told me in no uncertain terms that he and I were going to write a book about bunk beds. A particularly cool L-shaped bunk bed in my book had ignited his passion. After falling in love with that bed, the appearance of a lofted bed in a storybook was enough to make it a bedtime favorite. His eagle eye would spot bunks in home magazines and catalogs. If he found out that a friend had a bunk bed, oh man, we'd hear about it for weeks.

Finally, my husband and I said we'd begin the hunt for a bunk of his very own (even though he was still young for one). I created a Pinterest board and started a collection of images on Instagram to gather ideas. We dug up pictures of the bunks my sister and I slept in as kids. My husband told us stories about a cousin-filled bunk room at his family's summer retreat. Whenever friends came over my son would ask me to show off our digital collection of dream bunks. Kids and grown-ups alike have loved weighing in on the possibilities.

Along the way, I discovered the wide world of bunk beds: short ones, super-tall ones, triple bunks, trundle bunks, bunks that look like full-blown forts! Beds perched in lofts and tucked into cozy nooks also popped up in our searches. It turned out that planning for my son's future bunk beds was joyful. At the same time, I couldn't help but notice that when magazines and websites wrote about my first book, editors would often ask about the rooms that featured—you guessed it—bunk beds. When I posted a photo of bunks from Benjamin Moore's annual color preview to my Instagram feed, it quickly became one of my most-liked photos ever (and that image now graces the cover of this book!).

I decided to order a book about bunk beds to further fuel our fun, but when I went to look for one, there were none in print. My son was right: We needed to write a book about bunk beds.

The Bunk Bed Book is a dream book: Inside you'll find 115 bedrooms from across the globe. Whether your tastes are traditional or totally eclectic, there is a bunk or a sleeping nook for you within. I hope this book will land on the shelves of decorators, designers, and my favorite bookstores, but I'd also love to see it tucked onto the shelves of kids' bedrooms and bunks. I hope it'll bring you some of the joy we experienced when we started to research bunks for my son.

The Bunk Bed Book is also a handbook. Picking bunk beds or designing them from scratch is a surprisingly intimidating task. (You should see my text messages and DMs from parents paralyzed by the choices.) And because bunks are often big investments, those decisions become even more fraught. I can't tell you exactly what to buy or build because it will depend on the space you have, but I can show you what worked for other families and even boutique hotels.

I've broken this book down into chapters based on the type of room, starting with Two's Company (classic two-bunk beds). From there, we explore Loft Beds & Cozy Nooks, Room for Three, Bunk Rooms, and finally the fantasy rooms, Designed for Fun. In every caption, I've tried to offer you the essential information you need to know about a particular design. In some cases, I've done a deep dive on a room, looking at it from all angles and in exacting detail, so you can see exactly how the room came together.

In the final chapter, Practicalities, you'll also find some key resources. I give you the rundown on bunk heights, mattress sizes, bedding, ladders, lighting, and more. I've also shared some of my favorite sources for ready-made bunks. I hope all of this will give you the confidence you need to create the bunk room of your own dreams. —LAURA FENTON

A BRIEF HISTORY OF BUNK BEDS

Before they were a feature in shared kids' rooms, bunks were more commonly the realm of sailors at sea. To fit more men into a vessel, beds would be built stacked one on top of another (and still are today). Illustrations and drawings of the belowdecks quarters of large ships show bunks dating back centuries. Bunked berths remain the bed of choice on trains, ships, and even submarines to this day.

In the seventeenth century in Europe, beds were often enclosed in cabinetry (either freestanding or built into the home). These so-called "box beds" offered many advantages: They gave some privacy to the sleeper in a one-room house; they helped hold heat in at night, keeping the bed warm; and occasionally they even separated sleepers from domesticated animals that might be inside a house during times of extreme cold. Some box beds were built with a second bed stacked on top of the main bed as a place for children to sleep: These were a very early type of bunk.

Clever carpenters surely built lofted beds into all manner of homes throughout history, but bunk beds proliferated with the dawn of the Industrial Age when they could be mass produced in factories. By the early 1900s mass production of furniture was well established in North America and Europe, and bunk beds were being produced by the thousands. Manufactured bunks can be seen in photos of turn-of-the-century hospitals, dormitories, barracks, and prisons. Space-saving bunks became the bed of choice for these types of institutional settings.

However, it seems it wasn't until the middle of the twentieth century that bunks became popular for families to purchase just for the fun and convenience. Boomers were the first generation for whom a bunk bed was a common fixture of childhood bedrooms. Over the intervening decades, furniture manufacturers have explored all the possibilities of bunk bed living, from stacked triple bunks to queen-over-queen mega bunks. Today, the possibilities are endless.

WHY CHOOSE A BUNK?

If the question is not what bunk to buy or build, but whether you want a bunk at all, let me persuade you of a bunk bed's many charms. Stacked and loft beds are both practical and playful—and, best of all, they can be both at the same time. Here are seven reasons to opt for bunk beds.

1 **BUNKS SAVE SPACE.** With a bunk bed you can fit two beds (and sometimes even three) in the floor space of one. If you opt for a loft bed, you open up the space below for studying or playtime.

2 **BUNK BEDS GIVE KIDS ROOM TO PLAY.** Even in shared rooms where space is not limited, a bunk bed can be a smart choice because it frees up more of the room for playtime.

3 **BUNKS ARE COZY.** There's something about being enclosed that just feels comforting. Again and again when I interviewed families for this book, parents would tell me that their children used their bunks as a place to retreat.

4 **BUNK BEDS GIVE A ROOM A FOCAL POINT.** From a design perspective, a bunk bed automatically gives a room more architectural interest and a focus for the design.

5 **BUNKS ARE FOR EVERYONE.** They're a favorite for kids' rooms, but bunks are for all ages. In my research, I turned up an apartment with a loft bed that belongs to a seasoned design editor and a gorgeous guest room outfitted with bunks for visiting grandparents.

6 **BUNKS SAY VACATION.** If you're outfitting a holiday home, bunk beds are an allusion to camp and lazy summer days. (And a bunk room is a fantastic way to pack in the cousins.)

7 **BUNK BEDS ARE FUN.** Almost every kid loves a bunk bed because they are a world unto themselves. With the help of a child's imagination, a bunk quickly becomes a house, a fort, a sailing ship, and more.

CHAPTER 1
TWO'S COMPANY

The most common and more basic type of bunk is two stacked single beds. (It's what is called to mind when we think of a "bunk bed.") Ready-made bunk bed options are many, with varying heights, styles, materials, and costs, so there is sure to be a bunk bed to suit your particular needs. Custom and built-in twin-over-twin bunks are also common—and relatively easy to construct, especially if your builder eschews tricky staircases. In these pages you'll find everything from what might be the world's most popular bunk bed to a genius closet-to-bunk conversion that will make people say, "I wish I'd thought of that!" Explore the many different ways designers and homeowners have stacked one bed on top of another to find inspiration for your very own bunk built for two.

oh-so-versatile white

Painted white bunks are a popular choice because there is no need to match the bed to the other wood elements in the room. The white color is like a blank canvas for the rest of the room. This sweet girl's room proves that a basic white bunk can be anything but boring when paired with mix-and-match patterns. Here a wall of star-patterned wallpaper acts as a playful, yet calm backdrop to the bunk bed, while the vibrant animal print on the Roman shade draws your focus.

This bedroom by Oliver Freundlich showcases a clever pairing of off-the-shelf furnishings: a ready-made white bunk bed and leaning desk. The desk makes an excellent partner for the bunk because its shape echoes that of the ladder and it uses the vertical space in the room like the bunk does. An Eames rocker and a rustic rag rug give the room an eclectic vibe.

White bunks pop against vivid emerald walls in this room designed by Emily Butler. With the high contrast between the walls and furnishings, Butler was restrained in her use of patterns, utilizing one bold print on the shade and throw pillows and a subtle check on the sheets.

In a room with complicated architecture, a simple bunk is often the best choice to fit in two kids because a significant portion of the wall space is unusable. In this bedroom designed by Studio Four NYC, a medley of textiles, including a suzani, patchwork quilt, and crocheted blanket makes the simple beds into a focal point of the room.

small-space solutions

When describing this petite child's room, designer Keren Richter of White Arrow says the room functions a bit like a Swiss Army knife. The secretary desk flips up when not in use; the armoire opens up with storage for books, toys, and clothing; and the bunk has a large storage drawer beneath the bottom bunk. Richter was drawn to the bed by Oliver Furniture, a Danish brand, because of its rounded shape and fully integrated ladder, which allow for the maximum amount of space to walk around the bed in the small room.

When Polly Hall and her architects at Open Haus Design were trying to figure out how to fit their family of four into a 1,030-square-foot house, bunks were an obvious solution for the kids' bedroom. The L-shaped design leaves the window uninterrupted to let maximum daylight in. The upper bunk was built by a carpenter, but the lower bunk was assembled from storage pieces from IKEA. When the family welcomed a third child after the renovation, there was even room for a crib on the wall opposite the window.

Positioning twin beds in an L shape leaves the center of a room open for play and other activities. However, an L arrangement requires a lot of uninterrupted wall space. These clever homeowners figured out how to save a few feet and fit in two beds by stacking one bed over the foot of the other. Genius!

When blogger and author Erin Boyle was trying to fit two kids into a one-bedroom apartment, bunk beds were the obvious answer. She opted for a model with an integrated ladder from Ouef that coordinates with both natural and white-painted woods. After her third child was born, the family sought out a larger home but brought the bunk beds along to make the most of the kids' play space. Upcycled wooden crates provide storage beneath the bed.

When Angie Wilson, the blogger behind *House Becoming Home*, set out to design bunk beds for her son and daughter, she had two goals in mind: to pack in more storage and to free up more space for play. By building the beds in an offset design, she was able to contain them to one wall of the room. Placing storage drawers and cabinets below eliminated the need for dressers, so the kids have the rest of the room free for activities. And that trippy pattern on the wall? It's fabric! Wilson added it for a playful punch of pattern.

ROOM TOUR:

GRANDPARENT BUNKS

BEFORE A TOP-TO-BOTTOM MAKEOVER, Los Angeles designer Dee Murphy's only spare room was a self-described "catchall of crap." A queen-size bed filled the narrow room. When Murphy decided to renovate, she explored many ways to make the space work better. Her designer's mind turned to bunk beds, but Murphy's most frequent guests are her own parents—and bunk beds are not a conventional choice for senior citizens. Murphy asked if they'd be game to sleep in bunks and with their blessing, she moved forward with her plan to create the ultimate granny suite.

CONTINUE THE TOUR →

EAMES FURNITURE

THE KINFOLK HOME

the COVETEUR

BRIAN GLUCKSTEIN

"Don't be
afraid of
color and
pattern in a
small space.
You can go a
little wilder."

—DEE MURPHY

Murphy's advice for anyone considering bunk beds for an adult guest room is to think hard about how you can add functionality to a piece that you are building. In Murphy's case, the backside of the bunks was built with a clothing rail and shelves where her parents could hang things up. Within the bunks Murphy added spots to put water and books. Take your time to figure out what everyone's needs might be, and plan out every inch of space, says Murphy.

A bold green paint job and Milton & King wallpaper on the ceiling were purely decorative choices that turned the room from forgotten into a show-stopper.

Another key element to the renovation was to make the closet an extension of the room: Murphy removed the closet door and designed the California Closets built-ins to be seen, so that the closet feels like an alcove, not a separate, closed-off space. Continuing the green paint and wallpaper into the closet were key to making them feel like part of the room as a whole.

something bold on the wall

In this room by designer David Netto, a simple white bunk bed looks sophisticated against a backdrop of Quadrille toile wallpaper. To further envelop the room, Netto used the same pattern for the curtains. Vintage Poul Kjærholm armchairs up the sophistication in this child's space.

Decorator Emily Butler created a city bedroom that is a modern nod to the forest. Birch tree wallpaper covers one wall while the other three are painted a rich, verdant green reminiscent of the color of the forest canopy. If you want to position a bunk bed with only the head against the wall like Butler did, be sure to invest in a well-made, sturdy model like this metal one from Room & Board.

Designer Bachman Brown employed a confident, limited color palette to make this boy's bedroom feel as designed as the rest of the home. The map wallpaper on the wall behind the bed gives the room interest and dimension and elevates the simple Oeuf bunk. Brown repeated stripes in the window treatment, floor tile carpet, and tie-dyed bed linens to add to the visual punch without overwhelming the room with patterns.

curtain cues

For this Tahoe family retreat, interior designer Brittany Haines of ABD Studio designed the daughters' bedroom with sleepovers in mind. The full-size bunk beds have checked privacy curtains hung on tracks, which can be pulled shut for darkness or privacy.

These simple bunks get style flair from short, polka-dotted curtains. The setup would be easy to replicate for many bunks: A curtain wire supports metal hooks with clips that hold the fabric (IKEA sells affordable versions of this type of wire and clips). The curtains themselves require no fancy sewing, just straight hems—easy!

Nashville decorator Ashley Gilbreath has developed something of a specialty converting closets into built-in bunk beds. It all started with her own vacation home where she was trying to squeeze in as many sleeping spots as possible (and she figured that guests rarely make use of a large closet). Gilbreath says it's a relatively easy conversion for a carpenter as long as you have enough room to fit the bunks. She likes to add curtains to bunks for privacy, especially when there are additional beds in the room.

The curtains steal the show in this alpine bunk room designed by the team at Bonesteel Trout Hall, who turned classic wool Pendleton blankets into drapery. Not only do they add color to the white and wood space, but the heavy wool keeps the kids' sleeping nooks cozy when the temperature drops.

Workstead, a New York–based architecture and design firm, created this shared bed-room for a family who planned to stay in their apartment long-term. They wanted a room that would grow with their children and provide the maximum amount of space to play. To accomplish this task, Workstead, a firm known for their cabinetry and millwork, decided to transform the room's 6 x 6-foot closet into bunk beds; they also pushed into part of a hall closet to create a built-in dresser. The rest of the furnishings, a large armoire and a desk, are also built-in, leaving the center of the room open for playtime.

Opposite: The steps up to the bunk each have a storage drawer with kid-friendly cutouts instead of knobs.

Top right: Integrated curtains made from Rebecca Atwood fabric can be pulled shut for privacy and darkness.

Bottom right: The wall-to-wall desk has spots for two kids to study.

a focal-point ladder

For this custom bunk, the homeowners used plumbing fixtures to create a quirky climb to the upper bunk. Narrow ledges at the head and foot ends of the beds make a space for kid collections and their latest books, and two deep drawers underneath provide storage. The guardrails are also constructed from plumbing parts (a long length, a short length, and an elbow).

When Sara Story Design created bedrooms for siblings for this family home in Singapore, the firm opted for custom bunks. In each room, a ladder painted a bright color in high-gloss lacquer creates a natural focal point, making the ladder almost look like a piece of art against the white or neutral wood bunks.

When Karen and Conrad Allen set out to renovate the centuries-old cob barn on their property, they planned to rent it out as a part of Venn Farm, their luxury vacation rental in north Cornwall. So, naturally, they had family accommodations in mind. The Allens' personal style leans toward white walls with pops of color, but Karen notes that children are naturally drawn to primary colors, which is why they opted for the bold red ladder and Componibili storage unit by Kartell.

When designing this bunk room, the Allens' goal was to create a sleeping solution that would not interrupt the clerestory windows that run the length of the second floor. The windows dictated the height of the bunks, and they added a slightly smaller trundle beneath the lower bunk.

crossing
a window

In this bunk room by Robert Young Architects, a wall of bunk beds is built around an existing window. By centering the minimalist ladder opposite the window, the window lets light into all four bunks and no one has to worry about the open window being immediately adjacent to their mattress.

Designer Dana Small placed a double-over-double bunk in front of a window in her Michigan summer home. The white-painted nickel gap wood reflects the window's light.

Andrew J. Howard didn't let a window stop his plans for a bunk bed in this compact room. To make it work, Howard designed the bunks to bisect the window. What might have been an awkward design turned into a charming detail, especially with the wood painted in a bluebird hue. Hinson's iconic "Splatter" wallpaper adds a playful vibe, while two wall-mounted guard sconces are a practical choice.

step
right up

One of the first choices you need to make when designing or purchasing a bunk is whether you want steps or a ladder. Andrew J. Howard opted for steps on the bunks in his own children's room. Here the steps and lower bunks are built with drawers. The campaign-style drop-pull drawer handles are a wise choice for the stair drawers. They lie entirely flat so they don't impede climbing, but lift up when you wish to pull the drawer out!

If you have room (and the budget), steps offer several advantages: Casa Kids founder Roberto Gil points out that they're easier to climb for kids and grown-ups alike, they often have storage drawers in the steps, and they're a little safer than a ladder. Jamie Bush + Co. used one of Gil's beds as the centerpiece of this stylish children's room.

These bunks designed by Katie Ridder are a feat of carpentry with drawers built into each step of the stairs. The handsome guardrail not only adds a decorative touch, but the scooped-out center makes it a little easier to make the bed. Another idea to steal: Fabric upholstery inside the bunks gives each bed a cozy, warm feeling.

classic style

Decorator Tom Scheerer employed a host of preppy details to make this bunk room feel like summer, including pom-pom-bordered curtains, ticking stripes, and a vintage fan. The antique ladder is a quirky choice to access the upper bunk.

Located in an oceanfront home, Scheerer took his inspiration for this small bedroom from ships' quarters. The mattresses of the bunks and the daybed are upholstered in a crisp stripe. Nautical art and a vintage campaign-style dresser reinforce the subtle seafaring theme.

black and white

Black and white is almost always right. In fact, it is a signature palette for Sissy + Marley Design, a New York-based design firm with a knack for sophisticated kids' rooms. In this boy's room, they show how black and white can create a room that grows with a child. The black rug grounds the space, while the birch furnishings offer subtle warmth.

In another room by Sissy + Marley, a single black wall defines the study area from the rest of the room. Just a few yellow accessories pop in the monochromatic room and show how easily just a few colorful additions might totally change the feeling if and when a child craves a new look.

To keep black and white from looking too cold, bring in natural elements like wood, seagrass, or living plants like designer Jean Liu did in this hip take on a beach-themed bedroom.

simple and sophisticated

A smattering of toys reveals that this room belongs to a young inhabitant, but designer Shawn Henderson has created a space that is as chic as a boutique hotel with handsome woods and a grown-up palette. Located in a city apartment, Henderson made use of the available space by building bookshelves into the headboard and a desk (just barely visible here) into the foot end. A slim ladder and window seat leave the rest of the floor space open for play.

Vacation vibes abound in this chic sleep space. The white-on-white scheme of the room is contrasted with a dark, almost-black ceiling color. It's a surprising and bold choice that grounds the room while leaving it feeling airy. A traditional staircase leads up to the upper bunk, and the homeowner used the awkward space below to create shelves and a place to hang clothes.

Leave it to a fashion designer known for laidback luxury to create a kids' room that feels grown-up yet easy-going. In Jenni Kayne's children's room, white and blond wood fur-nishings create a serene backdrop for toys while textured touches like a pendant light, vintage rattan chair, and mounted antlers add interest.

the world's most popular bunk bed

W henever parents go looking for an affordable basic bunk bed, they're often led to IKEA's Mydal, a classic wood bunk that has been in the catalog for years. Mydal is beloved not just for its low price, but also its ability to be customized. Whether through playfully patterned sheets or paint—or both!—Mydal is a style chameleon that can be used just about anywhere.

Opposite: Blogger and entrepreneur Jordan Ferney demonstrates the power of paint in her sons' former bedroom in San Francisco. The IKEA bunk beds had at various times been painted red, orange, and black. They're seen here in their final minty hue before the family moved to the East Coast.

Top right: Mydal works brilliantly as part of this colorful kids room designed by Saudah Saleem. The green paint job bridges the sunny yellow walls and the bright blue of the rug's stripes.

Bottom right: Painted a pale gray, made up with white linens, and accessorized with vintage finds, Mydal looks laidback and minimalist in the home of West Coast writer Chantal Lamers.

BUNKS TO THE RESCUE FOR A FAMILY OF NINE

WHEN ZOË KIM AND MATT PAXTON married, their combined families became a blended family of nine. Kim has four kids from a previous marriage, and Paxton has three boys from his first marriage. All seven children live with the couple except when they are visiting their other parents. It's the definition of a full house. Fitting nine people into 2,700 square feet sounds like a math problem from a standardized test, but it's one Kim and Paxton were uniquely equipped to solve. Kim is the author of *Minimalism for Families* and Paxton was a featured expert on the television show *Hoarders* before creating his own show, *Legacy List with Matt Paxton* on PBS.

CONTINUE THE TOUR ⟶

In the main house, Kim's two younger boys share a room with a bunk bed and her older two share another room with traditional beds. The results are a surprisingly min-imalist family home that has a special place for every child.

The secret to creating their new home lies in tapping unused space, downsizing their stuff, and investing in three sets of bunk beds that fit all the kids.

Kim and Paxton made use of the unused space above Kim's garage. A full renovation transformed this into two bedrooms and a bathroom for Paxton's three boys. Working with the unfinished space enabled them to build custom bunks into the eaves of the roof.

EXPERT ADVICE:

TIPS FOR SHARED ROOMS

When I was an editor at a parenting magazine, my boss never wanted to run any stories about shared kids' bedrooms because she believed that very few kids shared rooms anymore. Statistically, she was not wrong: American houses keep getting bigger and families keep getting smaller. However, in my real life, I know plenty of families who have their kids share bedrooms, especially in cities, where space is at a premium.

Even out in the 'burbs, families will often choose to have kids share a room. My sister and I shared until we hit our tween years—even though the house we grew up in had a whopping five (!) bedrooms. My parents, like many others, hoped sharing a room would help deepen the bond between their kids and also teach them a little bit about problem-solving and compromise.

Designing shared kids' rooms is tricky because every kid, family, and home is different. When I was researching and writing this book, I saw so many different solutions for shared kids' rooms. What works for one family might not work for another—and that's okay! When you're looking for ideas, try to zero in on families with very similar circumstances to your own: same number of kids and spread between ages, a comparable type and size of home, and similar life needs. Through my interviews with other parents, here's what I have learned about shared room success:

1 **MAKE THE ROOM A SLEEP HAVEN.** As soon as children start sharing a room, they start waking each other up! If you haven't already outfitted the kids' room with blackout curtains and a white noise machine, these may help increase your odds of both kids sleeping through the night.

2 **SYNC UP THE SLEEP SCHEDULES.** Aim to get your kids on the same sleep schedules, so you can do bedtime routines and read stories together. If there's a big age gap between your kids, try separating their bedtimes by at least one hour to cut down on the chaos.

3 **FREE UP THE FLOOR SPACE.** Put the beds or bunks against the walls instead of sticking out into the room to maximize space. One of the reasons bunk beds are so popular for shared rooms is because they open up the floor for playtime.

4 MAX OUT YOUR STORAGE— ESPECIALLY CLOSETS. A whole host of shared room troubles can be solved by installing ample storage and giving each item a designated home. People often think of custom closet systems for the primary bedroom, but you may get even more value out of custom storage in a shared kids' bedroom.

5 CREATE PLACES FOR "SPECIAL" THINGS. Find a way for big kids to store their precious items away from a younger sibling, like a high shelf for complex LEGO creations or a cabinet where the Hatchimals are out of reach. If you opt for bunks, a ledge or shelf near the foot end of the top bunk area is a great idea.

6 GIVE THEM EACH THEIR OWN SPACE. As kids get older, it's important for each child to feel like they have their own space within the room—even if that's just the immediate area around their beds. Bunk beds are a great choice because they offer each kid a personal, semi-enclosed space.

7 CREATE A RETREAT. Bunk beds naturally give each kid a feeling of separate space, but you can enhance that feeling of privacy with curtains (turn to page 30 for curtain inspiration). For regular beds, a bed tent or canopy can do the same. You can also use floor-to-ceiling curtains on a hospital track to divide a room.

8 MAKE THE BEDROOM FOR SLEEPING AND QUIET TIME. If you find your kids fighting about how their room is used, consider designating the bedroom as the place for sleep and quiet-time play or study. This will mean that the more active playtime is happening in your living room, but it may be worthwhile to cut down on squabbling. During the pandemic I heard about a family who rearranged their home so the kids started sharing one room for sleeping and used the other bedroom as a playroom—and they liked it so much, they kept it that way!

9 TRY BEDS THAT DISAPPEAR. If you're committed to a small, shared room for the long haul, Murphy beds or Murphy bunks might be a worthwhile investment. Turn the page to see how these foldaway beds let the kids have the full use of the room during the day for playtime and then come out for sleeping at bedtime.

Finally, I want to note that sometimes it makes sense *not* to share a room, if that's an option. My friend Shira Gill, a professional organizer, had her two girls sharing a room and was using her home's small third bedroom as a home office, but when her older daughter campaigned for her own room, the whole family swapped rooms to give the girls their own spaces. Shira now works at the dining room table and says the loss of a dedicated office was a small price to pay for sibling peace. When designer Shavonda Gardner and her wife downsized from 2,400 square feet to a 1,200-square-foot two bedroom, they still let their preteen and teenage kids have their own rooms and converted the den into a third bedroom for themselves. Being flexible and nimble like that is the key to living in small spaces.

murphy bunks

Bunk beds are an incredible space saver, giving you two beds where you can usually fit only one, but wall beds (commonly known as Murphy beds) give bunks a run for their money with their fold-down design. Combine the two concepts, and you've got what is perhaps the ultimate space-saving sleeping solution: Murphy bunk beds.

When designer Elizabeth Reback's clients tasked her with renovating their loft to accommodate visiting family without dividing up the space and losing its loft-y feeling, she had to get creative. One of her clever solutions was turning a wide hallway along a bank of windows into a disappearing bedroom for the grandkids with a pair of Murphy bunk beds.

Decorator Celerie Kemble is best known for residential and hotel design where space is rarely a consideration, but for this New York City family, she employed Murphy bunk beds from Resource Furniture to give her clients' son extra playing space. The walls are painted white to make the room feel bigger, and Donghia's "Splatter" wallpaper on the ceiling adds a playful touch.

Interior designer Jacqueline Schmidt made room to breathe in her two sons' 10 x 11-foot bedroom with foldaway bunk beds from Resource Furniture. Jacqueline had her contractor build a soffit above the beds for an almost seamless, built-in look. (There is also a cabinet at the left of the beds.) A small oak desk, a play table and chairs, a cot, and wall-mounted storage complete the room.

For one New York City family living in a two-bedroom apartment, decorator Melinda Orlie-Katsiris had to figure out how to turn the 14 x 13-foot room into a shared space for a kindergartner, a middle schooler, and a high schooler. Murphy beds were the answer.

In Orlie-Katsiris's design, one side of the room got a pair of Murphy bunk beds and on the other a single wall bed. Both beds feature dual functionality with desks that fold down when the beds are stored. The desk surfaces cleverly stay horizontal, so you can even leave a laptop or schoolwork there when you pull down the bed. The desk on the bottom of the bunk side can comfortably seat two.

When Alison Mazurek started her blog, *600sqftandababy*, she was a new mom hoping to make her one-bedroom apartment work for a couple more years after the arrival of her baby boy. Little did she know she'd end up welcoming a second baby and staying until her eldest was seven years old before finally moving on to larger digs.

Mazurek and her husband gave their baby the bedroom and installed a Murphy bed in the living room for themselves. However, after their daughter was born, space was once again at a premium. Mazurek decided to invest in more Murphy beds: this time bunk beds. When they purchased the beds, their son was still only four and too young for the top bunk, so they had him sleep in the lower bunk (his sister was still in a crib) until he was a little older.

Top right: When the beds are closed, they only take up just over a foot of space in the bedroom, allowing for the most space for play.

Bottom right: The small 8 x 9-foot bedroom sits just off the dining/kitchen area with two doors leading into the room.

CHAPTER 2

LOFT BEDS & COZY NOOKS

Part of the allure of a bunk bed is the feeling of enclosure. So, let's take a slight detour from stacked beds to examine single beds that are a world unto themselves: lofted beds, enclosed sleeping spots, and all kinds of cozy nooks. Designers and architects often create that same cozy feeling when they tuck a bed into a nook, sometimes carving space out of parts of a home that would otherwise go unused, like the space beneath the roof eaves or under a dormer window. These tucked in spots are so universally loved that the authors of *A Pattern Language*, Christopher Alexander, Sara Ishikawa, and Murray Silverstein wrote, "We have noticed a rather strong urge to give the bed a nook of its own—some enclosure." Apparently nooks strike a chord in people!

a nook with a view

Tucked under a steep roof peak, this serene sleep spot is built to fill the negative space beneath the eaves. A closer look at the simple design reveals a bedside bookcase against the exterior wall, drawers built in beneath the mattress, and a little ledge for glasses or a glass of water on each short end of the bed. Shutters offer a feeling of safety when the window is open.

Up under the attic eaves of an old Victorian home, designer Robin Henry created a sweet ▶ retreat for an almost-teenage girl. The full-size bed fits neatly into a dormer window. Curtains and a valance further frame the space and separate it from the rest of the room.

The bedroom in this California cabin feels like a verifiable treehouse thanks to a large picture window, a rustic wood ceiling, and a bed that almost fills the space. An actual treehouse is visible in the trees outside.

Living and working in the Bay Area, designer Kelly Finley knows a thing or two about small spaces. To make the most of these windowed bed nooks in two different homes, she packed in storage below the beds and coated the woodwork in brightly colored paint. Cheerful patterns on the bedding and window shades add a sense of delight to these cozy corners.

elegant
enclosures

Inspired by antique box beds, the custom berths in this Baton Rouge home by architect Bobby McAlpine and designer Ray Booth are the epitome of Scandi-chic. Luxe linen curtains and cashmere throws complete the elegant styling.

An elaborate archway surrounds this bed nook in a home in Marrakesh. The deep blue-green walls play up the contrast between shadow and light in the windowed enclosure.

Designed with napping in mind, this boxed-in single bed sits in a dressing room in designer Philip Mitchell's home. The curtains darken the space during the day and absorb sound to make it quieter. The slim drawers below hold Mitchell's partner's extensive tie and pocket square collection! The bed linens and curtains nod to antique textiles without being period pieces.

Designer Amy Munger created this ladylike room for her niece, who had fallen in love with a bed with curtains while on a ski trip. Munger delivered her dream by creating two full-size sleeping alcoves hung with curtains sewn from a Quadrille fabric. A budding writer, Munger's niece loves to cuddle up in her nook when she works.

The Jennings is not your average hotel. Self-described as "equal parts accommodation and art project," the Jennings's owner Greg Hennes invited his creative friends to design the rooms. So instead of room after room of the same furnishings, each space has its own personality. Shelter Collective, an Asheville-based firm, divided this studio into sleeping and living spaces with a wall with an arched opening. Almost all of the room's furnishings are built-in for a feeling of simplicity.

The simple platform makes the sleeping area visually connected but physically separated from the rest of the room. The raised platform also eliminates the need for a bed frame or side table and doubles as a chair to sit on and tie your shoes.

Deep teal paint and a mustard-hued curtain lend the room depth.

daybed dreaming

Decorator Nick Olsen proves that you need not be afraid of pattern or color in a cozy nook. Here an Albert Hadley print enlivens the ceiling while red upholstery makes the daybed cushions pop. The pillows can be moved aside to turn the nook into a sleeping spot.

▲

Designer Andrew J. Howard created a magical retreat with this daybed centered around a window. Here a dark, almost moody green envelops the space. Simple shelves built into either wall provide welcome storage for books and other curios.

◀ There's nothing like an enclosed daybed for cozy reading or an impromptu afternoon nap. Howard decked out this light, bright nook with an inviting mix of prints and patterns. Beadboard paneling is a low-maintenance wall finish that gives the room texture.

study spots

W hen Erin Feher and her husband Danny renovated their San Francisco apartment, it was a do-it-yourself affair. With the help of Erin's dad, Erin and Danny moved walls and rebuilt rooms to carve out two bedrooms in just 550 square feet. Because they had poured so much sweat and tears into the space, the couple brought in professionals for some elements, including the desk and closet area under their daughter's twin-size loft bed from California Closets.

When commissioning custom storage, remember to build in flexibility, especially in kids' spaces. For example, as Erin's daughter grows, she can remove the lower clothing rod to accommodate longer dresses.

Their California Closets designer put the desk on the back wall to create a break between the closet side and the study side of the bed. The shallow shelves above the desk are backed with pink-painted glass for a pop of color.

In this bedroom, the desk is built right into the bunk, a clever way to max out the space without it feeling like the furniture is crammed together. The plywood wall panel visually separates the "study" zone from the sleeping area. The custom-made bed to the right has a lower bunk at a right angle.

In this narrow room, Roberto Gil, the founder of Casa Kids, created a custom loft bed that creates a bridge across its young inhabitant's space. The setup creates three distinct zones in a very small room: one for play, one for study, and one for clothing storage and getting dressed.

blush nooks

It's no surprise that this peony-pink corner is in the home of fashion designer Tracy Reese, who is known for her fearless use of color. The so-called "kitty cat room" is a narrow loft space tucked above the stairs. Simple white curtains offer the sleeper a hint of privacy, and built-in storage nooks below hold textiles and some of Reese's magazine archives.

Designer Amy Sklar decided to make the bed the focal point of a small room. With no room for a traditional dresser, Sklar built drawers into the bed platform and stairs and designed a bedside table with drawers. To give the nook a tailored look, Sklar had the curtain fabric paper-backed so it could be used as wallpaper inside the nook. The upholstered pelmet conceals the track for the curtains.

Inspired by both Japanese tansu chests and Swedish box beds, architect Tom Stringer designed this beautiful bed niche with several clever features. In addition to the storage beneath the bed, the center set of "drawers" is actually a false front attached to a set of steps that pulls out. To make the bed easier to change, Stringer designed the bed platform to sit on extra-large drawer glides, so it can be pulled out from the wall. Fretwork adds a decorative detail around the bed opening.

When designer Brooke Wagner realized she had enough room to create toe-to-toe twin beds in this shared girl's bedroom, she decided to create what she calls a double daybed. The floating beds are surrounded by padded upholstery to create a cozy feeling.

CHAPTER 3

ROOM FOR THREE

S ometimes a two-bed bunk is not enough. Luckily, when you need room for just one more, you've got a dizzying array of options. This chapter explores all the ways you can fit three in a bunk or bunk-and-bed combo, including single-over-full beds, stacked triple bunks, and clever L-shaped configurations.

stacked three high

igh-gloss blue paint makes this triple bunk pop, and extra details in the mill-work make it a true design focal point. The designers continued the equine wallpaper behind the bunk for continuity.

Joni Lay's lucky daughters have a room away from home at their grandparents' house. To fit three of her four daughters in one relatively small room, Lay opted for a triple-decker bunk, which she purchased online. The integrated ladders take up the least floor space possible. Lay's signature vintage finds and graphic patterns dress up the basic bunk.

When families have three kids, high ceilings, and not a lot of space, custom bunk builder Casa Kids will encourage their clients to consider a triple bunk. Although this bunk for three looks like a built-in, it is actually a piece of furniture, which meant the family was able to disassemble it when they moved. Steps make the ascent to the top bunk less intimidating.

Built to fit three kids, this stack of three bunks features a space-saving design in which the footboard is the ladder. Note how the beds are just narrow enough to not obstruct the room's window. If you have a similar space where a regular twin doesn't fit on the wall between a window and a corner, check to see if a European or RV-size mattress will fit. Here, simple lengths of metal pipe act as guardrails for the upper bunks, and a large rolling drawer offers storage underneath.

In this ski house by Workshop/APD, an epic three-bed bunk is more like a part of the architecture than a piece of furniture. Built from white oak, Workshop/APD's design gets gradually smaller on each level: The base beds are queens, the second level is a full, and the top is a single.

Right: There are integrated drawers with leather loop pulls across the bottom for storage.

Opposite: Ample landing space and slanted stairs with handholds make climbing easier and more comfortable.

single over double

In this sweet and chic bunk by Casa Kids, steps lead up to a twin bed that hovers over a double. Casa Kids' signature plywood design keeps the look simple to grow with the child. A pileup of pillows and hits of hot pink give the room some spunk.

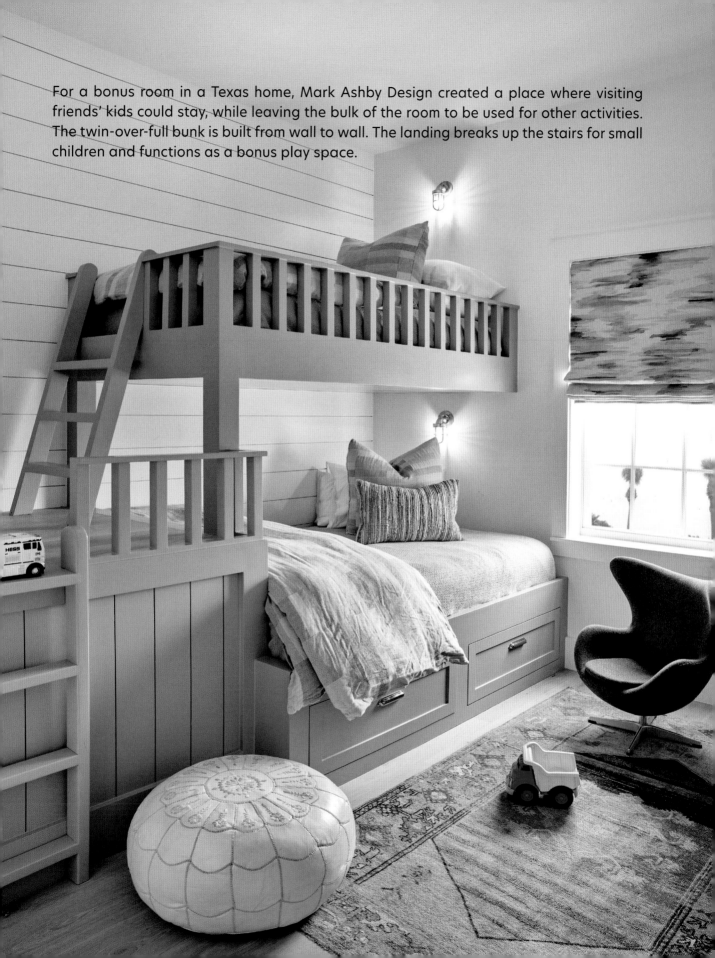

For a bonus room in a Texas home, Mark Ashby Design created a place where visiting friends' kids could stay, while leaving the bulk of the room to be used for other activities. The twin-over-full bunk is built from wall to wall. The landing breaks up the stairs for small children and functions as a bonus play space.

Mom of two and designer Erin Gates used a similar design formula for two bedrooms designed for brothers to avoid either feeling jealous of the other's room. For both she opted for a single-over-double bunk paired with colorful walls, simple Roman blinds, and a quietly graphic rug underfoot. Gates says she likes to make kids' rooms fun but also not too juvenile, so they can grow with the child.

T-shaped arrangements

When a single bed is lofted over lower beds to create a T-shaped arrangement, the upper and lower beds are most often separate pieces. This gives homeowners welcome flexibility for how the furniture might be used in the future. This custom bunk by designer Shawn Henderson uses a slatted wood design to create a feeling of enclosure for each bed while letting light and air pass into the spaces. The top bunk is high enough that a desk could easily fit in the lower space if the children later have their own rooms.

A single bed lofted over a double creates an ideal arrangement for a guest bedroom because it lets parents and a child or three kids share a room. This bed is clad in nickel-gap paneling, which has a farmhouse vibe, but sophisticated sconces and textiles elevate the look.

A sense of play is palpable in the room of jewelry designer Maria Duenas Jacobs's daughters. The design team at Thé Cappiello created a loft that seems to float above the two twin beds below, thanks to the dreamy clouds painted onto the wall and the luminous Murano glass chandelier.

ROOM TOUR:

1 BUNK, 1 MURPHY, 3 NOMADIC KIDS

WHEN MURAL ARTIST RACHEAL JACKSON went to redesign her kids' shared bedroom, she'd already experimented with a single-over-double bunk, but she wanted to better maximize the floor real estate, which led her to the idea of a Murphy bed. In the redesigned space, her kids, ages seven, six, and two, have a fort-like bunk bed on one side of the room and a queen-size Murphy bed on the other for a total of four possible sleep spots. Jackson describes her kids as nomadic sleepers, saying it's always a surprise where they will find them in the morning!

Top left: The fanciful bunk is constructed from basic 2 x 4s and plywood that Jackson embellished with 1 x 2 slats. She also snuck in five drawers underneath for extra storage.

Bottom left: The red ladder steps are actually sturdy towel bars that Jackson spray-painted and mounted as steps.

CHAPTER 4

BUNK ROOMS

Bunk rooms call to mind summer camp and cozy ski cabins. They are a smart choice for maximizing space in a holiday home where guests will be spending less time in their rooms. But bunk rooms can also be an everyday solution for families with multiple children or who often host guests. Whether you are buying bunks or building out a customized room, there are many options for configuration and styling.

the power of a pair

Two Restoration Hardware bunk beds *just* fit along the wall in this girls' room designed by Josh Greene and Katrina Hernandez. Because the bunks can be configured with either right- or left-hand ladders, they were able to center them for a pleasingly symmetrical design. The weathered woods act as a foil to the sweet wall color.

For this shared girl's bedroom, M + M Interior Design turned off-the-shelf bunk beds from Pottery Barn into something more special with the help of floor-to-ceiling curtains. The red-bordered pelmets conceal the basic track hardware for the long drapes, which, in addition to creating design drama, offer each sister a little additional privacy for her bunk.

In a children's guest room by DHD Architecture and Interior Design, the wildly popular bunk beds from Oeuf are positioned catercorner to one another and dressed in block-print bedding and pillows. Bold red stripes on the walls and ceiling give the room a joyful, carnival vibe.

built-in beauties

To make a strong color work in a narrow bunk room, consider using it for (almost) everything. Here, designer Suzanne Kasler painted the beadboard, moldings, window trim, and every part of the bunk all in the same glossy blue.

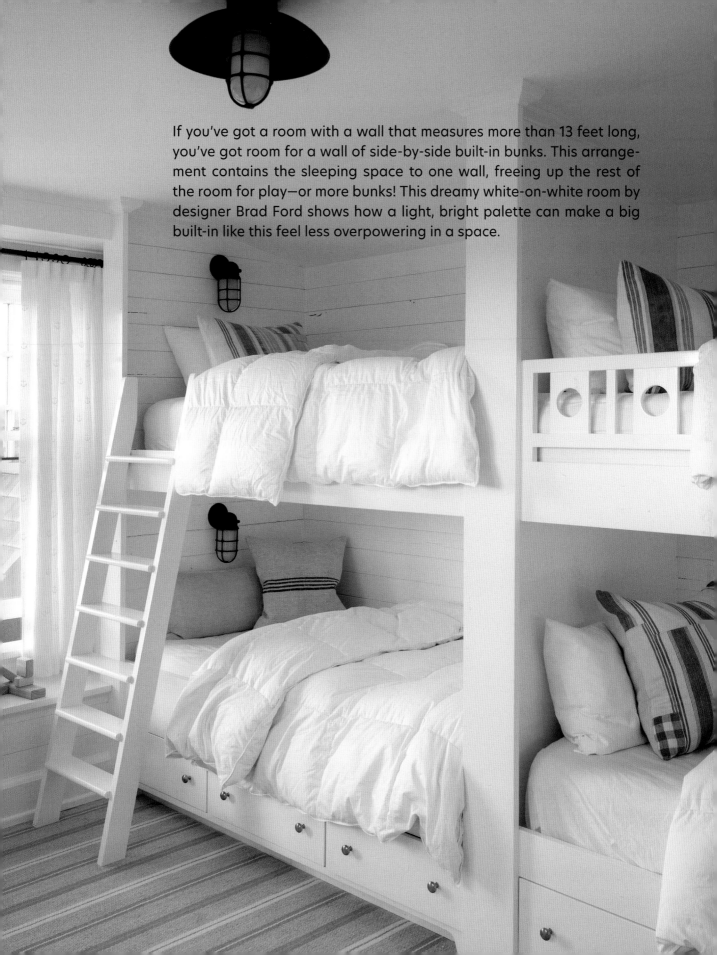

If you've got a room with a wall that measures more than 13 feet long, you've got room for a wall of side-by-side built-in bunks. This arrangement contains the sleeping space to one wall, freeing up the rest of the room for play—or more bunks! This dreamy white-on-white room by designer Brad Ford shows how a light, bright palette can make a big built-in like this feel less overpowering in a space.

Designer Brooke Wagner fitted this bunk room out more like a boutique hotel than a campground cabin. Here the entire bunk bed wall is padded and upholstered for a cozy feeling and sound dampening. The lower bunks sit just a few inches off the floor to give both berths ample headspace. The open, integrated ladders let the maximum amount of light and air into the lower bunks.

For this Lake Tahoe home, Liza Reyes created bunks with a classic style. The clean-lined design and blue and white palette feel both on-trend and timeless. Individual sconces mean everyone can control their own lighting.

A long narrow room becomes a kids' paradise in the hands of Australian design firm The Designory. The high-ceilinged room was ripe for a loft bed, and the designers settled on a toe-to-toe design with an angled ladder leading to each bed. A net built into the loft lets daylight from the skylight reach the lower beds and also provides the kids with a playful element. The ladders can be moved, so the trundle bed can be pulled out when there's a full house.

A bunk room lets the guests pack into this two-bedroom lake house in upstate New York. The vintage-style ladders hook onto the upper bunks. Mismatched blankets give the space a charming vibe.

cabin-inspired quarters

CLB Architects prove that an all-wood interior need not be rustic or country. For this mountain retreat, they used rift-sawn white oak to create a sleek bunk room. A minimalist ladder and railing made of metal complete the streamlined design.

Wood and bunks go together like peanut butter and jelly, so it's no surprise that designers often turn to wood paneling for bunk rooms. In this fresh take on a cabin interior, natural wood paneling covers the walls, ceiling, and even the door. Fresh prints and bright colors give a lift to the design.

Well known for their use of natural wood, California-based Commune Design lined this whole house with locally salvaged Monterey cypress—both inside and out—in part because it will develop a natural patina over time. The bespoke bunk room pairs the wood with patterned curtains that reflect the blue-centric palette from the rest of the house. Nearly invisible storage drawers below the bed offer clothes storage.

Above: Elsewhere in the house, Commune built a daybed into a window. With the bookshelf placed immediately beside it and a wall-mounted sconce above, this corner is an ideal spot to while away an afternoon with a good book.

These two bunk rooms are located in one narrow house in a seaside retreat designed by UK-based Ham Interiors. The tall home required some creative solutions to make the most of the available space. Custom bunks let the kids pile in. The "boys' bunk" and the "girls' bunk" sleep a total of seven. There is storage tucked in beneath the beds. The design team included quiet nods to the home's locale, like guarded sconces and nautical stripes in the design.

pattern play

Interior designer Elena Frampton opted for built-in bunks as an efficient way to fit three brothers into one room in a Manhattan apartment. Each bunk features a different curtain textile, giving each some distinction and personality. The blue-stained woodwork, custom brass railings, and Tracy Kendall wallpaper lend the room an elegant feel.

Interior designers Peter Dolkas and Michelle Ficker of Studio Dorion had fun dressing the bunk room in this weekend home. They used two tones of bright blue paint on the bunks and floors and added red wall sconces to each berth. A base of pale blue sheets on each bed allowed them to play with slightly mix-and-match pillows and bedspreads.

EXPERT ADVICE:
CREATE AN IDEAL
SPACE FOR GUESTS

Chances are, if you are setting up a bunk room, you are
planning on welcoming guests to your home—possibly lots of them. A great guest room
requires more than a place for your friends and family to sleep. Here are a few ways you
can make their stay more comfortable and keep your house tidier while they're there:

1 **GET HOOK HAPPY.** Hooks are a guest room's best friend. They give your guests a place to hang their coats, purses, bath towels, damp swimsuits, and more. You really can't have too many hooks in a guest bedroom, but aim for a minimum of one hook per person.

2 **PROVIDE AMPLE SPACE FOR THEIR STUFF.** Yes, it's tempting to use the guest room's closet and drawers to store your off-season stuff, but be sure you've left enough room for your guests to unpack their clothes. Keep all horizontal surfaces, like dresser tops, completely clear, and leave enough space on a closet shelf or floor for their luggage (having this out of the way will make their room feel less cluttered).

3 **MAKE THEM COMFORTABLE.** Offer guests a variety of pillows and blankets to choose from, in case they prefer to be warmer or cooler than your own family. All you need are a few extra blankets and a spare pillow or two in the closet, plus a verbal invitation to your guests to grab what they need. (Pssst... If you're hosting young children who may still wet the bed, be sure to show the parents where the clean change of sheets is located, so they don't have to wake you in the night.)

4 **DON'T NEGLECT THE BEDSIDE.** Each bed or bunk needs its own light and some kind of nightstand or shelf. This way your guests can read or relax in bed comfortably. Bonus points if their bedside reading lamp

is on a dimmer so they can control the brightness.

5 **COLOR-CODE YOUR TOWELS.** When you've got a full house, it can feel impossible to keep track of whose towel is whose. Mark each towel in some way to help everyone out. This could be a different colored towel loop sewn onto each towel or even a simple dot drawn onto the corner of each towel with a variety of colored permanent markers.

6 **HELP THEM RECHARGE.** In our modern day almost every guest will arrive with a device—if not three. Set your visitors up with a power strip and a charger. You'll also do them a favor by posting the Wi-Fi network and password somewhere convenient, so they don't have to ask you for it every time they log on a new device.

CHAPTER 5

DESIGNED FOR FUN

Bunk beds are inherently fun, but some are more playful than others. From a simple slide to a tree-house-like design, we'll explore ways to make a sleeping space into something absolutely joyful. However, what you won't find in these pages are bunks shaped like pirate ships or Disney-themed rooms. Hyper-specific designs leave no room for children to grow and evolve. To prevent today's bunk from becoming tomorrow's trash, this chapter focuses on fun, but open-ended designs.

slide right in

Jane Bonsor, the founder of London-based textile company Korla, created an indoor play space for her children with a bunk from Germany's Woodland Bunk Beds and a bevy of plus-size beanbags and floor pillows made from her Korla fabrics.

For this family home, Andrew J. Howard designed custom bunks to fill two walls. A slide ▶ creates a playful exit from one of the top bunks. Mirth Studio wooden floor tiles are a pretty and practical flooring choice for a kids' room that's built for fun.

tent tactics

For his television show *Build Me Up*, Orlando Soria redesigns rooms in a hurry and on a budget. This child's bedroom shows off his resourcefulness. Here a standard IKEA loft bed is reimagined as a camping-inspired tent. Soria had a carpenter build an A-frame structure right onto the store-bought bunk and then stitched and stapled a canvas cover on top. The simple but bold wall graphics and hanging swing seat give the room a further sense of play without breaking the budget.

architectural interventions

G lobe-trotters can stay the night in a fantastical bunk room at the BnA (Bed and Art) Hotel Akihabara in Tokyo. Not your usual traveler accommodations, BnA is a social and artistic project that aims to support Japanese artists while providing travelers with the unique experience of staying in what is essentially a piece of art. This room by studioBOWL was imagined as an "activity park"—complete with a fireman's pole to exit the upper bed.

This narrow room demonstrates how a few architectural interventions can completely transform a space. Here a lofted bunk bed is enclosed by panels of plywood with strategically placed cutouts. The interior of the bed is painted in a deep shade of blue that gives the space an extra feeling of depth. The primary palette adds to the kid-like feeling in the space without being too juvenile. A simple pulley and rope mechanism lets the kids raise toys up to the bunks.

Opposite: Cutaways in the plywood fronting create the ladder to the lower sleeping berth. A tiny rope ladder leads the way to the upper bed. Mesh nets line the "windows" to the sleeping berths as a safety precaution.

Above: The entrance to the kids' room is a kid-size door that gives the room a fun house ambiance. A second taller, but still pint-size door leads into the closet space. Openings with shutters let in light and air.

This colorful custom bunk was not Studio Ben Allen's first bunk commission. (You can flip the page to see another sleeping space they designed in the same building.) In this instance, the homeowners were looking for a way to stay in their beloved one-bedroom apartment now that they had become parents. The bunks were part of a larger apartment renovation that used built-ins to maximize the small space. Working with London-based Top Notch Joinery, Studio Ben Allen created a lofted bed with puzzle-like parts that move to accommodate studying and play.

Top left: The head of the bed is set into an arched niche with a little wall-mounted reading lamp within. A tall, narrow cabinet to the left of the bed creates clothing storage for the child.

Bottom left: The lower step to the bunk pushes in to create a child's desk, and the cheerful green lounge chair can be pulled out into the living room.

This modernist room design by Studio Ben Allen takes its inspiration from a surprising source: an early Renaissance painting, *Saint Jerome in His Study* by Antonello da Messina, which depicts a cardinal at study in an enclosure full of nooks, niches, and cut-out arches. Designed for an apartment in London's Barbican Estate, which itself has arches incorporated into the design, the room is shared by two siblings. Their dad requested space for them to sleep, relax, play, and study when they stay with him on weekends. Allen and his team created two interconnected but distinct spaces for the kids with the bunk bed itself dividing the room in two. Allen notes the structure is as much a piece of architecture as it is furniture. The structures are also multifunctional and movable: Desks and steps can be folded away or moved.

The peaked ceiling above each bed is a subtle nod to the berths being little houses for each child.

Constructed of birch plywood, the structure was designed so that it could be disassembled and moved, if needed.

closed-in quarters

Looking at her children's rooms, you can tell that designer Jessica Davis doesn't take design too seriously. When she set out to create the kids' rooms in her mid-century modern Atlanta home, Davis decided to use plywood to enclose basic, inexpensive loft beds she found online. Davis cut out the arches with a jigsaw, then she and her daughter painted the graffiti-style design on the bunk together. Not only do the lofts provide each child with a cozy place to play or read beneath the bed, there is a secret passage underneath her daughter's bed that leads into a cabinet in the family's den!

Davis used finished-grade plywood, which has a smooth surface for her children's bunks, noting she says she loves the look of modern plywood furniture with the exposed laminated edges.

Sarah Sherman Samuel has a knack for capturing the design zeit-geist ahead of the curve. Case in point: A simple idea to enclose her son's bunk beds in MDF with cutout arches launched hundreds of imitators. Samuel and her husband built the underlying bunk bed from 2 x 4s and plywood.

climbing walls

Instagrammers Sarah Randall and Kenna Valdez teamed up to make over a kid's room. The do-it-yourself bunk bed was sized to the existing mattress. To create the climbing wall, the women attached 2 x 4s to the room's studs. They drilled holes in the plywood for the rock holds and attached them to the plywood before mounting the plywood onto the 2 x 4s.

A ladder or steps is the usual way to reach a bunk, but brave parents might also offer ▶ their kids rock climbing holds, as well. Because the foot- and handholds will support your child's weight, you cannot mount them on drywall. Instead, they need to mount on studs or another sturdy base.

fantasy beds

An attic space becomes a nautical playground with the help of some marine building supplies. Thick rope is employed as a handrail for the stairs, supports for the beds, and even to hang an indoor swing! Meanwhile, the wood, chains, and hooks of the beds and trundles nod to a ship's design. With the trundles pulled out, this room can sleep eight!

Although most themed bunk beds are kitschy, one type of pretend-play bunk is open-ended enough to grow with children: house-shaped beds. Sold by most of the mid- and high-end furniture retailers, house beds are a playful addition to a child's room. A white house bed feels fresh and modern when paired with a mustard painted ceiling and drapes, black accents, and a mid-century modern icon.

A simple bunk is transformed into a castle with the addition of a few plywood cutouts. This is a smart strategy for a themed bed. The embellishments could easily be removed once the inhabitant is finished with her princess phase. The fantasy feeling of the room is enhanced by a strict palette of white and pale blue—and a full-size stuffed deer toy!

You'd be forgiven if, after touring this apartment by INC Architecture & Design, you concluded that the children had taken over the decorating. But the brief for the whimsical space came from the color-loving mom who craved an indoor-outdoor feeling for her children in their New York City apartment. Although not every architect would know how to integrate a "tree house" into a downtown loft, INC was game for the challenge. The results are a home that is playdate central for the five kids who live there.

Opposite: The boys' room features a plywood playhouse–bunk structure that features a climbing wall built into one side.

Above: The "tree house" sits in an open portion of the living space and is constructed from walnut, painted paneling, and steel. The surrounding walls are papered in Cole & Son "Woods" wallpaper to nod to the forest.

For the girls' bedroom, INC created a "park" with green rubber Pirelli tiles as "grass" and a structural column turned into a "tree." They also converted a closet into a play-house for the two sisters.

CHAPTER 6
PRACTICALITIES

B uying bunk beds is intimidating! As soon as I tell another parent that I have written a book about bunk beds, they almost inevitably want to ask me questions. I tell them that the right bunk will depend on the space they have, but there are some good rules of thumb to consider before you purchase, commission, or build a bunk.

what to know before you buy or build

Height: The right height bunk will depend on your room's ceiling height (and to a lesser extent its overall size). Store-bought bunks range from 50 inches tall for a low-slung bunk bed to as high as 93 inches for a stacked triple bunk, but most fall somewhere between those extremes. Headspace is especially important on the top bunk, since this is the harder bunk to make. You need at least 36 inches between the top of the upper mattress and the ceiling.

If your ceilings are anything less than 9 feet, you should probably be looking for a low bunk bed which is also a great choice for younger children and smaller spaces. However, think twice before choosing a low-to-the-ground bunk for a room that will regularly accommodate teens or grown-up visitors.

Bed size: Today, bunk beds come in all sizes from twin to queen (I did not turn up any king-size bunks in my research, but I'm sure there's one out there!). When choosing between a twin and an extra-long twin, know that twin-size beds are most comfortable for people who are under 6 feet tall. If your bunks will be used by taller adults, an extra-long twin or even a full-size bunk bed is the way to go.

Also consider how you will use the space. For example, some families will choose a twin-over-double for a shared children's room so there is plenty of room for two siblings and a parent to read stories together.

Mattress: Bunk manufacturers usually specify the appropriate mattress size. You need to know that your mattress height will impact your overhead space, and in a small space, the difference of a few inches can matter. Include the mattress height when making your calculations and consider a thinner mattress to maximize your space.

CONFIGURATION

Lofted: A lofted single or double bed can give you more usable space in a small bedroom. If the space below will be used as a desk, you can get away with just 54 inches of clearance, which is enough space for most adults to comfortably sit and work. However, if you plan to walk beneath the bed, you'll need to go even higher and consider something custom.

L Shape: An L-shape bunk offers a few advantages. They take up less floor space than two single beds, and in three-bunk models, you can fit in three kids without extra-high ceilings. However, you lose some of your space savings when you opt for an L over a traditional twin-over-twin.

T Shape: A popular choice for a guest bedroom, this style has a single bed overhead running lengthwise along the wall. The lower bed's headboard is against the wall and the footboard is the center of the room, creating a T shape.

Kids grow fast! Don't build in a toddler-size desk or art table; instead, opt for the adult-size desk and pair it with a taller-than-average "youth chair" to boost the child up until she grows into the desk.

Stacked Triple: Most stacked three-bunk beds stand about 92 inches tall. For a comfortable clearance on the top bunk, you'll need ceilings of about 10 feet tall or higher.

Flexible: Many manufacturers are building flexibility into their designs with bottom bunks you can add or remove, stacked twins that can be separated later on, and more. One of these might be pricier than a fixed bunk, but it could save you money in the long run when you don't need to buy additional beds later.

STORAGE

Many beds include storage drawers below the bottom bunk. It's a smart strategy for kids' toys or clothing. However, if you're designing a guest room, a pull-out trundle might be a better use of the space. If you have an existing bunk with no storage beneath, you can add a drawer designed to go under the bed or even plain wooden crates.

DAYLIGHT

The last thing you want is for your bunk to make your room less appealing, so it is important to consider how daylight flows into the room. A poorly placed bunk bed can obstruct the light. Always try to avoid placing a bunk in a position that will block views or light. Beds with open or slatted ends allow light to pass through the bed more readily than those with a flat panel. Likewise, a bed with stairs will block more light than one with a ladder.

When parents go to buy a bunk bed, they are often overwhelmed with the number of choices available, especially today when typing "bunk bed" into a search engine yields thousands of options. Here are a few guidelines to help you choose the right one:

Whenever possible, see your bunk beds in person before making a purchase. Lie down in the bunks, climb the ladder, give the whole thing a little shake to see how sturdy it is. This is the only way to truly get the feeling of a piece of furniture. The possibility to see it in person might even sway your decision toward a bunk you can see and touch and one you cannot.

If it's not possible to see a particular bunk bed in person, at least go look at *some* bunk beds and take the kids too. Bring along the measurements of the bunk you are considering buying and a tape measure to see if you can get a better sense of it. Measuring things like the height of the top bunk to the floor and the top of the lower mattress to the bunk overhead can help you visualize a bunk you can't see. And if there is something you hate about the bunk you see in person, take note.

Tape it out. Back at home, use blue painter's tape to mark out a bunk bed's silhouette in a room. And don't just mark its position on the floor, mark how high it will go on the wall. Pay attention to how close the bed comes to any fixed features like windows, closets, and doors, and make sure you have plenty of clearance to walk around the bed.

A WORD ABOUT
SAFETY

The American Academy of Pediatrics (AAP) recommends that children under six years of age should not sleep in bunk beds. If you buy a new bunk bed today, it will have been tested to meet your country's safety regulations. However, if you're purchasing a bed for your child secondhand (or building one), follow the AAP's guidelines: Elevated beds of all kinds should have rails or walls on all four sides. However, lower bunks with mattress foundations that are 30 inches or less from the floor do not need guardrails. The tops of the guardrails must be no less than 5 inches above the top of the mattress. The entrance to the bunk should be narrow: In the U.S., it can be no greater than 15 inches; in the U.K., it's just 11.8 inches (30 centimeters). AAP also offers these guidelines for how to place the bed in the room:

1 **PUT BUNKS IN THE CORNER OF THE ROOM** so that there are walls on two sides for extra stability.

2 **INSTALL A NIGHT-LIGHT NEAR THE LADDER OR STEPS** for visibility at night.

3 **IF IT IS NOT FIXED, SECURE THE LADDER** so that it will not slip.

4 **CREATE A HOUSE RULE** that bunk beds are not for roughhousing.

5 **REMOVE DANGEROUS OBJECTS** from around the bed.

6 **NEVER HANG CLOTHING,** belts, scarves, or ropes from the bunk bed, as they pose a strangulation risk.

EXPERT ADVICE:
DON'T FEAR THE CEILING FAN!

You can have bunks and a ceiling fan; you just need to make sure that the beds are a safe distance from the fan's spinning blades. If an existing fan is a little close for comfort, consider replacing the fan blades with shorter ones. Or if the fan has a downrod, swap out the whole fixture for a style that hugs the ceiling more closely.

LADDERS & STEPS

Steps versus a ladder is one of the first decisions you'll need to make when purchasing or commissioning a bunk bed. There are pros and cons to each. Here are some things to know as you decide on a ladder or step style.

Integrated straight ladders: The most common kind of bunk ladders, these go straight up and down and are affixed to one side of the bed. This type of ladder requires no additional floor space, and many bunk beds can be ordered or assembled to whichever side you prefer. This is also usually the most affordable option.

End ladder: Bunks with the ladder positioned on the short end leave the entire lower bunk open, which can be especially nice for adults and creates a more minimalist look.

Angled ladders: Less common than a straight ladder, an angled ladder

sticks out into the room. You want one with an angle of 30 degrees or less. Ideally, it should have a safety rail. These take up more room than straight ladders, but they are a little easier to climb.

Stairs: Steps are the easiest to summit and safer than ladders, but they also take up a lot of space. If storage is built into the steps, this can alleviate the need for a dresser, so that might make the extra cost and space worthwhile. Bunk beds with stairs are the priciest option.

BEDDING

There is no denying that making a bunk bed is hard. So hard, that I joked this book should come with a warning sticker that told prospective bunk owners that bunk beds are rarely as beautifully made as they are in these photos. However, there are some tips and tricks that will help making the beds a little easier.

When it comes to sheets and blankets, think simple. The less there is to make, the easier it will be. If you're craving decorative flair, a throw pillow or bolster can add another layer of styling without making the actual bed-making any harder.

Duvets are your friend. A fitted sheet and a duvet cover are going to be much easier to make than a fitted, flat, and blanket will be. If you typically change to a quilt and flat sheet in the summer, consider a lightweight duvet instead.

Typical twin coverlets often have an excess of fabric to tuck in. Consider buying king-size quilts and splitting them in half. A seamstress can cut the quilt in half and finish the cut edge to match the others.

Tailor to fit. Tailor a twin-side coverlet to fit the mattress to cut down on the frustration of making the bed. A local seamstress or even your dry cleaner can sew in seams to create a box shape.

Use fewer, larger pillows. Think about upgrading your bunks to a king-size pillow, which will stretch the full width of the bed. The larger pillow looks tidy and it also gives the sleeper more space to prop herself up for reading.

If you already struggle with bed-making, consider bedding designed specifically for bunks. There are several brands, including Beddy's, that make bedding that zips up somewhat like a sleeping bag, making it easy to get the linens into place. (Or maybe just give the kids sleeping bags and call it a day!)

Embrace a relaxed look. If you're willing to accept that the bed will never have hospital corners, you might decide to fully embrace a decidedly bohemian look. Get playful with mismatched patterns for the top and bottom bunk and consider linen, which looks absolutely lovely rumpled and mussed.

LIGHTING

Illuminating a bunk can be a little tricky, but there is no need for a dim or dark bed. Of course, a flashlight or a headlamp will work just fine for nighttime reading, but a more permanent solution will make the room more inviting in the before-bedtime hours. You have several options to light up your space, from quick fixes to permanent installations.

Wall-mounted sconces are a smart solution for bunk beds. If you have the luxury to hardwire them, do. It'll be worth the extra electrical costs to not have cords and plugs in sight. Carefully consider the placement before hardwiring and make sure there's an easy way for the person in the bunk to turn off the light from bed. An electrician can install a multiway switch, so the lights can be turned on and off from both the bedside and the bedroom door. For extra safety, consider a guard sconce. With the glass enclosed in a metal cage, there's no danger of accidentally breaking a shade or bulb in bed.

Another option is plug-in wall-mountable sconces. These can be secured directly to your bunk or the nearest wall. Use nail-in cable clips to keep the cords tidy.

Clip or clamp lamps can be attached to the bed frame or a nearby shelf or table. These are often more affordable than wall-mounted sconces. (You can buy a basic clamp lamp at a hardware store for less than $10.)

String lights are a fun and affordable way to light a bunk. You can use self-adhesive clips to hang the lights. Drape them for a more bohemian look or string them up in tidy, straight rows. And don't just settle for a strand of plain Christmas lights. Explore all the fun novelty lights!

Battery-operated lights might be a necessity if no outlets are nearby or you have opted for a Murphy bed. In addition to the many camping lanterns on the market, a few manufacturers make stylish, portable LED lights.

One disadvantage of bunk beds is that it's often tricky to figure out where to put your usual bedside belongings. Traditional bedside tables work for some lower bunks, but the top bunk is a perennial challenge. Here are a few ways you can sneak in storage for those nighttime needs.

Simple shelf: A board and a couple of brackets will hold the basics like a book and a glass of water, and the options of sizes and styles are endless.

Floating nightstand: Wall-mounted nightstands can be hung immediately next to an upper bunk for a more substantial storage option. If you go this route, consider a pair (one for the top and one for the bottom) for a coordinated look.

Book ledge: Mount a slim, wall-mounted book ledge on the wall adjacent to either the upper or lower bunk. A great place to store books, you can also clip a lamp onto the rail, if needed.

Fabric caddy: Several manufacturers make bedside pockets to hold books and other bedside items. Or you could do what blogger Erin Boyle did and tie an affordable carpenter's apron to the guardrail.

Low stool: If your bottom bunk is too low for a bedside table, a simple wooden step stool can be a place to rest a lamp or book.

Cup holder: If a glass of water is the main concern, you might mount a wall-mounted cup holder like you'd find in a bathroom. There are also foldaway cup holders sold for use on boats that you could try.

Spill-proof cup: My son used his sippy cup at night long past his mastery of drinking from a real cup. The spill-proof top helped him get a drink at night without help. For older kids, you could put their nighttime water in a water bottle with a top or straw.

A NOTE ABOUT
PLACEMENT

Place any shelves
that will go within the bunk space near the foot end of the bed, so that if a book or object falls off the shelf in the night it will land on feet, not the sleeper's head.

SOURCES FOR READY-MADE BUNK BEDS

BredaBeds
Makers of Murphy bunk beds
bredabeds.com

Casa Kids
High-quality, ready-made and custom plywood bunks
casakids.com

Colorado Made Bunk Beds
Rustic, Western-style bunks
coloradobunkbeds.com

Crate & Kids
A variety of off-the-shelf bunks at midrange prices
crateandbarrel.com/kids

Flexa
Solid wood, Scandinavian designs
flexa-usa.com

IKEA
Affordable ready-to-assemble bunks
ikea.com

Matrix
A great source for unusual shape and size bunks
maxtrixkids.com

Oeuf
Maker of the popular Perch bunk bed
oeufnyc.com

Oliver Furniture
Danish designer bunk beds ideal for small spaces
oliverfurniture.com

Pottery Barn Kids
A wide selection of classic, midrange bunk beds
potterybarnkids.com

Pottery Barn Teen
Geared toward teenagers with many loft bed options
pbteen.com

Rafa-kids
Designer children's furniture from the Netherlands
rafa-kids.com

Resource Furniture
Transforming and Murphy bunks
resourcefurniture.com

RH
High-end bunks, including many fantasy bunks
rh.com

Room & Board
Maker of high-end, American-made bunk beds
roomandboard.com

Wayfair
An online retailer that sells bunks through a drop-ship model
wayfair.com

Woodland Kindermobel
Playset-like bunks made in Germany
woodland.de

FEATURED DESIGNERS & ARCHITECTS

PHOTOGRAPHY CREDITS

Karen and Conrad Allen, 38-39

Brittany Ambridge, 12-13

Amy Bartlam, 97

Mark Bolton, 163

Erin Boyle, 18

Ariadna Bufi, 124-125

Phoebe Chauson, 18

Paul Costello, 165 (bottom)

Roger Davies, 55 (bottom)

Peter Dolkas, 141

Elizabeth Dooley, 68-69

Shannon Dupre, 108-109

Pieter Estersohn, 24-25, 42, 80-81, 88-89

Flashpoint Collective, 92 (bottom)

Emily Followill, 158-159

Kirsten Francis, 11

Steve Freihon, 114-115

French + Tye, 154-155

Bess Friday, 79

Genevieve Garruppo, 26-27

Ryan Garvin, 100-101

Juan López Gil, 94-95, 107, 175

Tria Giovan, 116, 177

Laurey Glenn, 91

Matti Gresham, title page

Clay Grier, 111

Greg Hennes, 86-87

Michael Hunter, 84-85

Racheal Jackson, 118-119

Alexander James 74, 138-139, 146

Stephen Kent Johnson, 47, 82, 110, 132-133, 136-137

Tomooki Kengaku,150-151

Zoe Kim, 58-61

Max Kim-Bee, 44-45

Erin Kunkel, 56, 76-77

Francesco Lagnese, 48-49, 126

David Land, 43, 57 (top), 90, 106, 147

Chantal Lamers, 57 (bottom)

Joni Lay, 105

Michael J. Lee, 112-113

Sara Ligorria-Tramp, 148-149

Andy MacPherson, 130-131

Alison Mazurek, 5, 70-71

Joshua McHugh, 140

Chad Mellon, 128

Karyn Millet, 32-33

Matthew Millman, 134

Frank Oudeman, 40-41, 64

Eric Piasecki, 46, 75, 122, 129

Costas Picadas, 95

Paul Raeside, 55 (top)

Sarah Randall, 162

Marco Ricca, 50-53

Thomas Richter, 14-15

María del Río, 92 (top), 93, 173

Lisa Romerein, 31

Zeke Ruelas, 20-23, 142

Annie Schlechter, 36, 83, 117, 135, 152-153, 164, 166-169, 174

Suzanna Scott, 30

Sarah Sherman Samuel, 160

SEN Creative, 78

Michael Sinclair, 156-157

John Stoffer, 161

Sara Story Design, courtesy of, 37

Werner Straube, 98-99

Heather Talbert, 123

Dane Tashima, 28-29

The CONTENTed Nest, 165 (top)

Trevor Tondro, 10, 127

David Tsay, 104, 180

Simon Upton, 65

Frederic Vasseur, 17

William Waldron, 8-9, 54

Björn Wallander, 96

Weston Wells, 3, 16, 66-67, 143

Matthew Williams, 34-35

Angie Wilson, 19

acknowledgments

Researching and writing this book was a spot of joy in a dark year when the world was locked down. Thank you to my sweet son, William, who dreamed up the idea for the book and got me thinking about bunk beds.

I am so thankful to all of the designers, architects, homeowners, and photographers who shared their work with me! Special thanks are due to the team at Benjamin Moore, who shared the beautiful photo that graces this book's cover.

My biggest thanks are due to my husband, Weston, who helped me juggle our work and parenting schedules with grace and patience while we had no childcare and schools were closed. Weston, you are a true partner in life. Thank you also to my parents who pitched in when they could—and who planted the seed for this book with my own beloved bunk beds back when I was a girl!

Thank you always to my agent, Sharon Bowers: I feel so lucky to have you on my team. Jenna Helwig, thank you for cheering me on in this and all professional endeavors. Finally, gratitude is due to the Gibbs Smith team, especially my editor, Sadie Lowry, and art director, Ryan Thomann: Thank you for bringing this book into the world with me!

ABOUT THE AUTHOR

Laura Fenton is the author of *The Little Book of Living Small*. Her writing has appeared in many publications, including *Better Homes and Gardens*, *Country Living*, and *Real Simple*. She has been featured on leading home websites, including Apartment Therapy, Cup of Jo, and Remodelista. As the former lifestyle director at *Parents* magazine, Fenton has a special expertise in family homes. She lives with her husband, photographer Weston Wells, and their son in Jackson Heights in New York City. You can follow her on Instagram @laura.alice.fenton.